NOT JUST A STORY

AN EASTER MUSICAL FOR UNISON/2-PART CHOIR

ARRANGED BY
CLIFF DUREN, MARTY PARKS,
GARY RHODES, J. DANIEL SMITH,
MIKE SPECK AND STAN WHITMIRE

LILLENAS.COM

CONTENTS

Christ Is Risen

includes

Alleluia! Alleluia!
Crown Him with Many Crowns

Arr. by Marty Parks

*CD POINTS: Split-channel, CD:1-27; Stereo Trax, CD:28-54

*Words by CHRISTOPHER WORDSWORTH; Music by LUDWIG VAN BEETHOVEN.

*Words by MATTHEW BRIDGES and GODFREY THRING; Music by GEORGE J. ELVEY.

34
Unis.
an - them drowns All mu - sic but its own! A -
E A D A/E A4 2/E Esus E G2/A A A7
37
cresc.
wake, my soul, and sing Of Him who died for
D A/E D/F♯ G G2/F♯ E D/F♯ E/G♯
cresc.
40
Div.
f
thee, And hail Him as thy match - less King Thro'
A D/F♯ G D/F♯ Em7 A D D/F♯
f
CD: 3
CD: 30
43
all e - ter - ni - ty.
G Bm Asus A7 D D/C B♭sus B♭
cresc.

46 *Unis.* **f**

Crown Him the Lord of Life! *Div.* Who tri - umphed o'er the

E♭ Cm A♭ E♭/G A♭ B♭7/F E♭

49

grave; Who rose vic - to - rious to the strife For

B♭sus B♭ B♭/D E♭ B♭/D Cm E♭ F B♭/D A°/C

52

those He came to save. *Unis.* His glo - ries now we

B♭ E♭ Fsus F7 B♭sus B♭ E♭/G E♭ B♭/F E♭/G

55 *Div.*

sing Who died and rose on

A♭ E♭ A♭ C7/G F E♭/G F/A

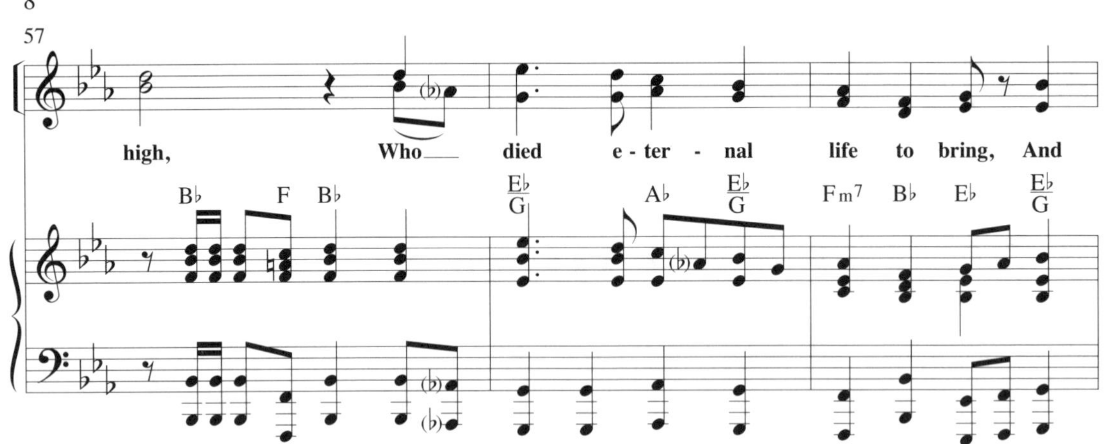
57
high, Who died e - ter - nal life to bring, And
B♭ F B♭ E♭/G A♭ E♭/G Fm7 B♭ E♭ E♭/G

CD: 4
CD: 31
60
lives that death may die.
A♭ Cm B♭sus B♭ E♭ E♭/B♭ Cm Dsus D

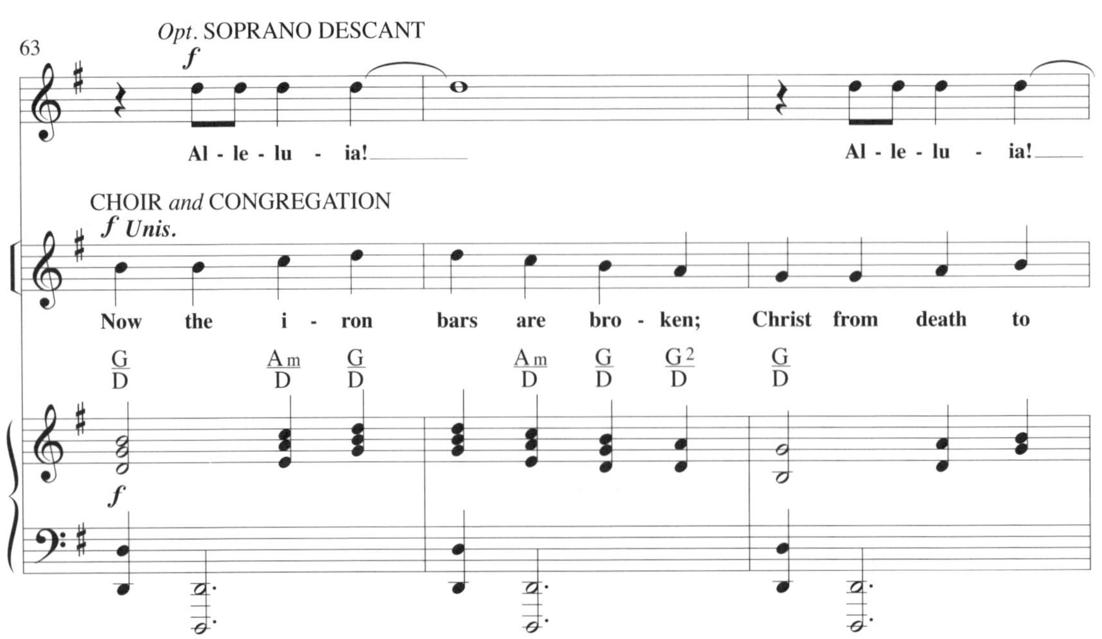
63
Opt. SOPRANO DESCANT
f
Al - le - lu - ia! Al - le - lu - ia!
CHOIR and CONGREGATION
f Unis.
Now the i - ron bars are bro - ken; Christ from death to
G/D Am/D G/D Am/D G/D G2/D G/D
f

66
Al - le - lu - ia! Al - le - lu - ia!
life is born– Glo - rious life, and life im - mor - tal
G/D D sus N.C. G F M7 C2/E G/E♭ C m6/E♭
69
Al - le - lu, Al - le - lu - ia! Al - le -
Div.
On this res - ur - rec - tion morn. Christ has tri - umphed,
G/D A m/D G/D D sus D G D(no 3) G/D
72
lu - ia! Al - le - lu - ia!
and we con - quer By His mighty - y en - ter - prise;
D(no 3) G/D D(no 3) B 7/D♯ E m7 A D

75
Al - le - lu - ia! Al - le -
We with Him to life e - ter - nal By His res - ur -
G Am/G G Am/D G/D D G
78
lu - ia!
ALL
rec - tion rise. Christ is ris - en!
Dsus D G FM7 C2/E Cm/E♭ Dsus
82
Opt. 3-part
ff
Al - le - lu - ia!
D Dsus D D7 N.C. G
8va
ff
fff

Not Just a Story

Words and Music by
RICHIE FIKE and
SEAN MULHOLLAND
Arr. by J. Daniel Smith

NARRATOR *(without music)*: Alleluia, Christ is risen! He is risen indeed. Down through the centuries the story has been told again and again. How God loved us enough to send His only Son to come and live among us. This spotless Lamb became the sacrifice that through Him, we might know the Father. *(Music starts)*

But it's much more than just a story of something that happened two thousand years ago. It's as real today as it was back then. The blood that was shed at Golgotha still covers our sins today. It cleanses us completely and reaches all the way to where we are.

11
Ev - 'ry tribe and na - tion sing "Our God is here!"
E♭
E♭/G
A♭2
13
Ev - 'ry tongue and spir - it, let the Fa - ther hear it,
E♭
E♭/G
A♭2
15
He is draw - ing near, let's sing "Our God is here!" And
E♭
E♭/G
A♭2
CD: 6 1st time
CD: 33 1st time
CD: 8 2nd time
CD: 35 2nd time
17
all of us, with all our hearts, are
B♭
C m

19
f
Div.
stand - ing up to say: It's not just a sto -
E♭/G
A♭2
21
Unis.
Div.
- ry, He rose from the grave. It's my tes - ti - mo -
E♭
C m
B♭
23
Unis.
Div.
- ny, I'm for - giv - en and saved. It's not some old fa -
E♭
C m
B♭
CD: 9 2nd time
CD: 36 2nd time
25
Unis.
- ble hand - ed down through the years. My God is will - ing and a -
A♭
B♭

2nd time to Coda
(to pg. 15, meas. 41)
Div.
- ble, might - y and sta - ble. It's not just a sto -
A♭
E♭/G
B♭
- ry.
E♭
A♭2
CD: 7
CD: 34
LADIES unis.
mf
In the small - est child,
in the deep - est tri - al,
On the long - est mile we see our

36
MEN unis.
mf
God is here.
In the midst of mer - cy,
E♭/G
A♭2
E♭
38
ev - en when we're hurt - ing,
He a - lone is wor - thy; yes, our
E♭/G
A♭2
E♭
D.S. al Coda
(to pg. 12, meas. 17)
CODA
40
ALL mf
mf Div.
God is here.
And - ble.
It's not just a sto -
E♭/G
A♭2
A♭
B♭
42
Unis.
Div.
- ry,
He rose from the grave.
It's my tes - ti - mo -
E♭
Cm
B♭
mf

44
Unis.
f Div.
- ny, I'm for-giv-en and saved. It's not some old fa -
E♭
Cm
B♭
46
Unis.
- ble hand-ed down through the years. My God is will-ing and a -
F
F
A
f
C
48
Div.
- ble, might - y and sta - ble. It's not just a sto -
B♭
F
A
B♭
C
CD: 10
CD: 37
50
- ry.
F
F
A
B♭2
F
dim.

53

MEN *unis.* *mp*

And all of us, with all our hearts, are

F/A B♭2 C D m

mp

56

LADIES *unis.* *mf*

stand-ing up to say: And all of us, with

F/A B♭2 C

mf

59

CHOIR *Div.* *f*

all our hearts, are stand-ing up to say: And

D m F/A B♭2

62

CD: 11

CD: 38

all of us, with all our hearts, are stand-ing up to say:

C D m F/A

f

65
sub.mp
It's not just a sto - ry, He rose from the grave.
B♭2
F
mp
67
It's my tes - ti - mo - ny, I'm for - giv - en and saved.
C
F
69
mf
It's not some old fa - ble hand - ed down through the years.
C
B♭
mf cresc.
71
cresc.
My God is will - ing and a - ble, might - y and sta -
C
B♭
F
A

73
f
- ble. It's not just a sto - ry, He rose from the grave.
B♭ C F D m
f
75
It's my tes - ti - mo - ny, I'm for - giv - en and saved.
C F D m
77
It's not some old fa - ble hand - ed down through the years.
C B♭
CD: 12
CD: 39
79
My God is will - ing and a - ble, might - y and sta -
C B♭ F/A

81
-ble. It's not just a sto - ry.
B♭
C
F
83
It's not just a sto - ry.
F/A
B♭2
F
85
It's not just a sto - ry.
F/A
B♭2
F
87
It's not just a sto - ry.
rit.
(6)
F/A
B♭2
F
F/A
B♭2
(3)
rit.

Settled at the Crossing

Words and Music by
LYN ROWELL, PHIL MEHRENS
and LEE BLACK
Arr. by Cliff Duren

NARRATOR: *(without music)* It's been said that once we truly see the cross, nothing else will ever look the same again. Our hopes and dreams, hurts and sorrows, and even our human insecurities all look different in the light of His love. *(Music starts)* It's a love that goes beyond all measure. Mere words can't explain it and our minds cannot comprehend it . . . but with our hearts we accept it.

8
Son.
Writ - ten there in crim - son, You
G♭2
C♭

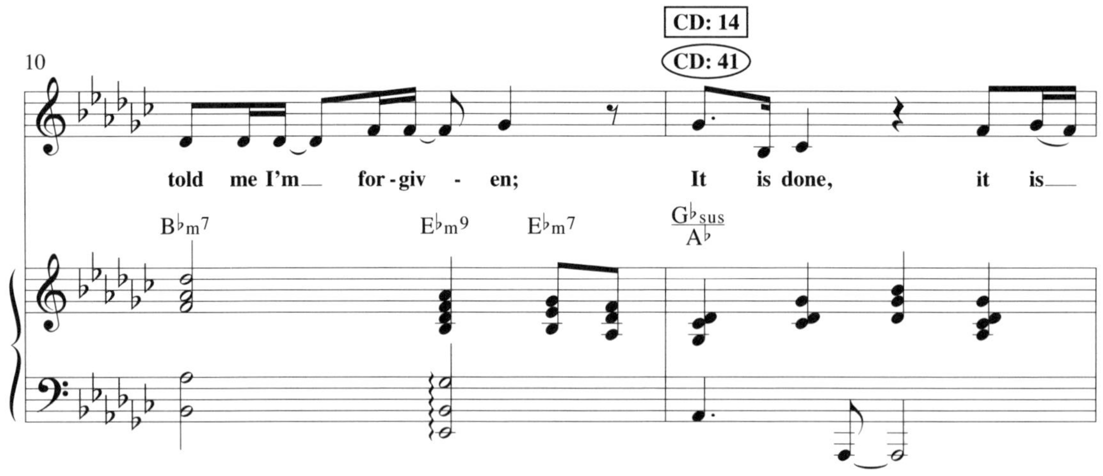
10
CD: 14
CD: 41
told me I'm for - giv - en;
It is done, it is
B♭m7
E♭m9
E♭m7
G♭sus
A♭

12
done.
So if You
nev - er speak an - oth - er word of
CHOIR
Unis. p
Oo,
D♭
F
G♭
B♭
G♭
C♭

14
blessing And the si - lence leaves me with a sense of
Oo,
G♭2
G♭/C♭
16
loss; I'll re-mem - ber if my heart be-gins to
Div.
G♭4/2
G♭
C♭
18
ques-tion, An - y doubt that You loved me
Unis. mp
An - y doubt that You loved me.
F♭m9
G♭sus/A♭

20
was set - tled at the cross.
Div.
Oo.
D♭7sus
C♭
D♭/C♭
CD: 15
CD: 42
22
G♭2/B♭
A
E/G♯
24
mp
I would be the first to ad -
Unis. mp
I would be the first to ad -
G♭2

26
mit I don't de-serve the kind of fa - vor You have al - ways
mit I don't de-serve
E♭m9
C♭
D♭/F
28
shown.
cresc.
But You don't have to tell me. You
Div.
cresc.
But You don't have to tell me. You
G♭2
C♭
3
cresc.
CD: 16
CD: 43
30
proved how much You loved me and I know,
mf
I'll still
proved how much You loved me
mf
I'll still
B♭m7
E♭m9
E♭m7
G♭sus/A♭

32
SOLO joins Choir
know. So if You
Unis.
know.
Nev - er speak an - oth - er word of
D♭sus D♭ G♭/B♭ G♭/C♭
mf

34
bless - ing And the si - lence leaves me with a sense of
G♭2 G♭/C♭

36
loss; I'll re - mem - ber if my heart be - gins to
G♭4/2 G♭ G♭/B♭ C♭

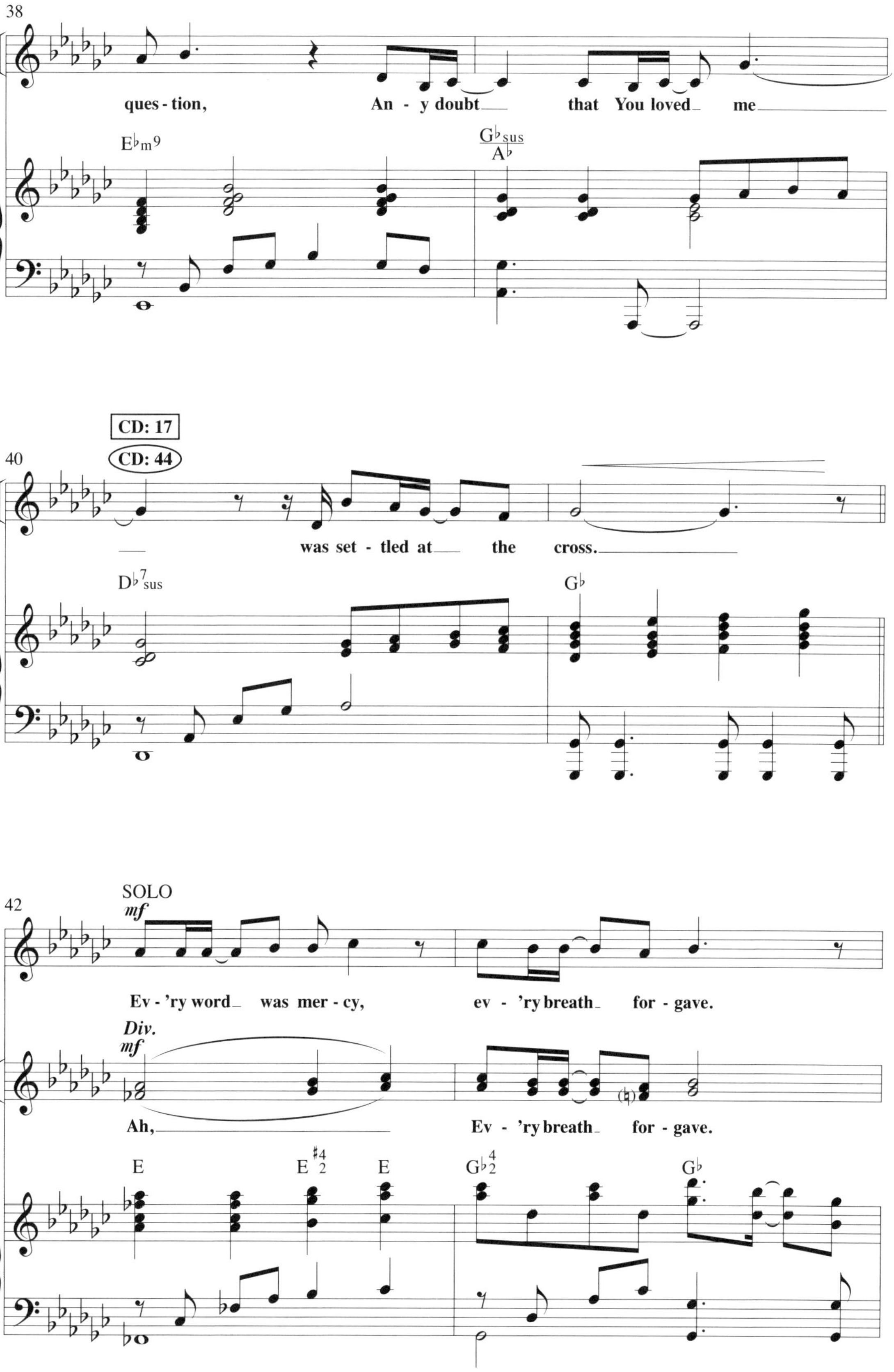

38

ques - tion, An - y doubt that You loved me

E♭m9

G♭sus / A♭

CD: 17

CD: 44

40

was set - tled at the cross.

D♭7sus

G♭

CD: 18
CD: 45
rit.
Ev - 'ry drop of blood testi - ti - fies of grace.
Tes - ti - fies of grace.
a tempo
Your grace!
If You nev - er speak an - oth - er word of
cresc.
O, And the si - lence leaves me,
bless - ing And the si - lence leaves me with a sense of

50
I'll re - mem - ber.
loss;
I'll re - mem - ber if my heart be - gins to
A♭4 2
A♭
A♭ C
D♭
CD: 19
CD: 46
52
An - y doubt that You loved me
Unis.
Div.
ques - tion,
An - y doubt that You loved me
F m9
A♭sus B♭
54
was set - tled at the cross.
was set - tled at the cross.
E♭7sus
D♭
D♭♯4 2
D♭
mf

56
mp
An - y doubt that You loved me
A♭/C
Fm9
A♭sus/B♭
mp
58
was set-tled at the cross.
p
Thank You, Je - sus.
E♭7sus
D♭
E♭/D♭
D♭
A♭2/C
61
molto rit.
p
(2)
At the cross.
Unis.
mp
Div.
An - y doubt was set - tled at the cross.
B
G♭/B♭
G♭ (3)
A♭
p
Ped.

Jesus Messiah

Words and Music by
CHRIS TOMLIN, DANIEL CARSON,
JESSES REEVES and ED CASH
Arr. by Gary Rhodes

NARRATOR *(without music)*: For He hath made Him *(music begins)* to be sin for us, who knew no sin; that we might be made the righteousness of God in Him.

10
Div.
Em - man - u - el.
The res - cue for sin -
E♭
B♭sus
B♭
13
- ners,
the ran - som from heav - en;
E♭
A♭2
16
CD: 21
CD: 48
Je - sus, Mes - si - ah,
Lord of all.
A♭2
E♭/G
B♭sus
19
Unis.
mf
All our hope is in You,
E♭
Fm7/4
cresc.
mf

22
All our hope is in You; All the glo -
E♭2/G
A♭2
B♭sus
B♭
25
- ry to You, God,
CD: 22
CD: 49
The Light of the
Fm4 7
E♭2/G
A♭2
28
world.
mp
Div.
Je - sus, Mes - si - ah!
B♭sus
E♭
dim.
mp
31
Name a - bove all names;
Bless - ed Re - deem-
E♭
A♭2

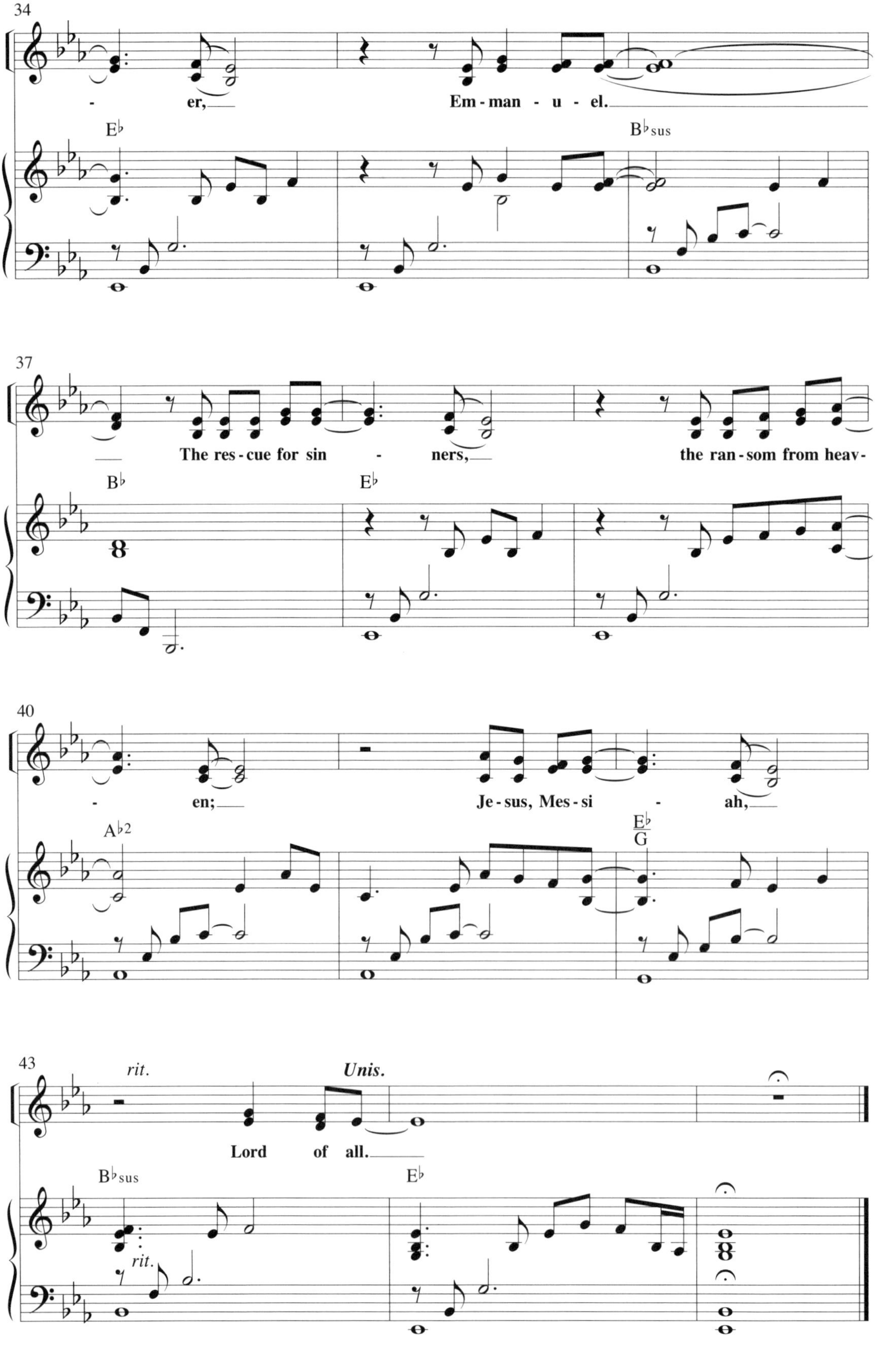

34
er,
Em - man - u - el.
E♭
B♭sus
37
The res - cue for sin - ners,
the ran - som from heav -
B♭
E♭
40
en;
Je - sus, Mes - si - ah,
A♭2
E♭/G
43
rit.
Unis.
Lord of all.
B♭sus
E♭
rit.

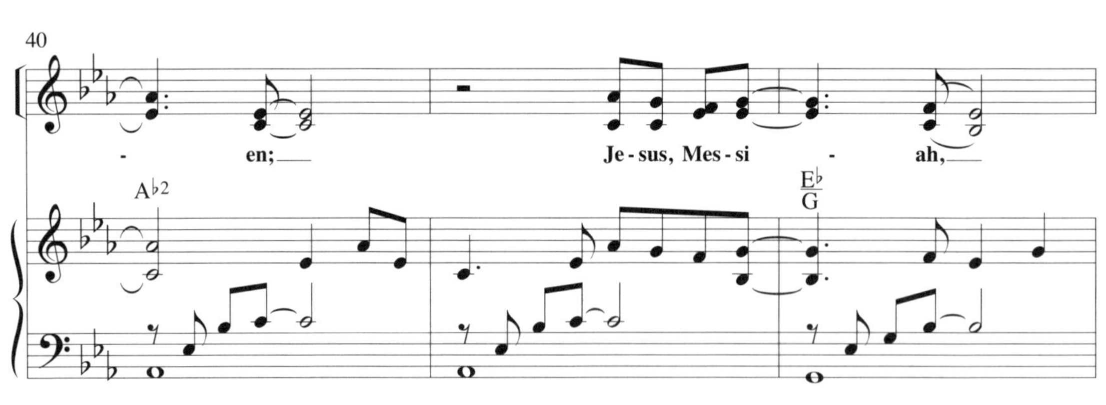

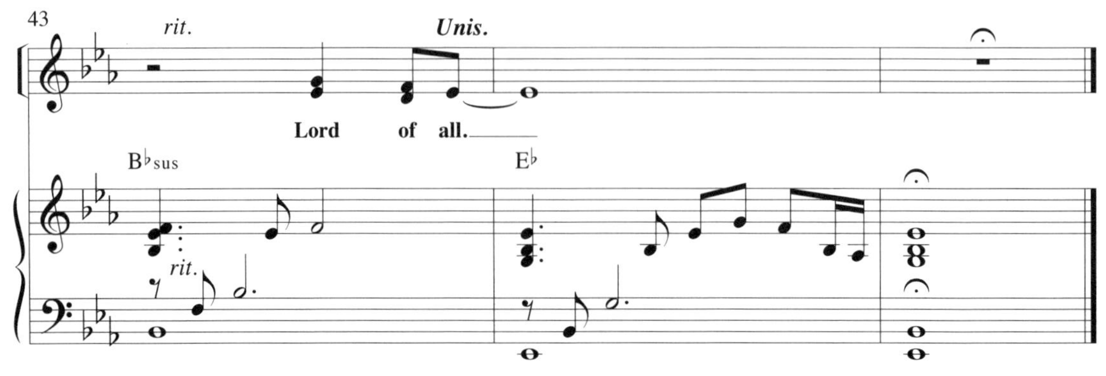

Christ Is Alive

includes

Because He Lives
Alive Forever Amen
Christ Arose
He Is Lord

Arr. by Mike Speck and Stan Whitmire

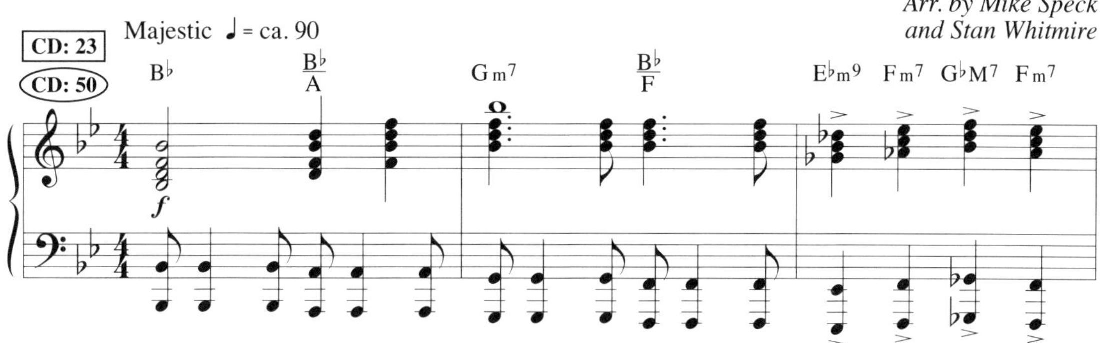

NARRATOR *(without music)*: He lived, He died *(music begins)* and He rose again. Through His grace we have been justified freely that we might come forever into His presence. This is the message of the cross!

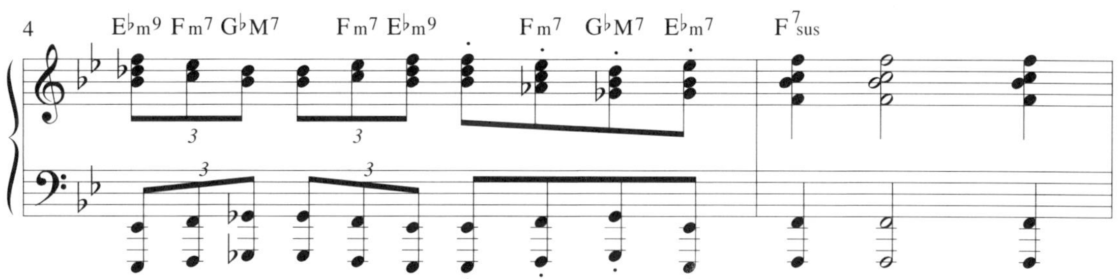

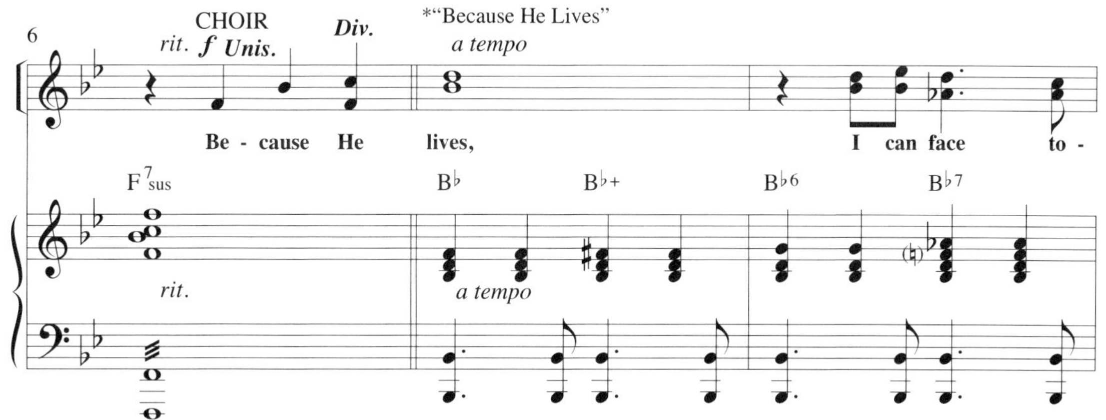

*Words by WILLIAM J. GAITHER and GLORIA GAITHER; Music by WILLIAM J. GAITHER. Copyright © 1971, renewed 2000 by William J. Gaither. All rights controlled by Gaither Copyright Management. Used by permission.

9
Unis.
mor - row; Be - cause He lives,
E♭ G7/D Cm E♭/F Dm7
12
Div.
Unis.
Div.
all fear is gone. Be - cause I
Gm Gm/F C/E Cm/F F♯°7
15
know He holds the fu - ture
Gm E♭m/G♭ B♭/F Fm7 B♭7 E♭ B♭/D B♭sus/C B♭
18
And life is worth the liv-ing– just be-cause He
A♭9 E♭m/G♭ B♭/F E♭/F B♭/F E♭/F D/F♯

*Words and Music by DAVID MOFFITT, SUE C. SMITH and TRAVIS COTTRELL.

31
hal - le - lu - jah. A - live, praise and glo - ry to the Lamb.
A♭2
E♭2
G♭M7
A♭2
33
A - live, a - live, a - live
B♭2
35
CD: 25 2nd time
CD: 52 2nd time
hal - le - lu - jah. A - live for - ev - er, a - men.
A♭2
E♭2/G
G♭M7
A♭2
B♭
37
1
(to pg. 37, meas. 30)
Div.
He's a - live,
B♭
2
B♭

*"Christ Arose"

39 *Unis.* — *Div.*

B♭ — B♭/A — Gm7 — B♭/F

Up from the grave He a - rose, With a

41

E♭2 — Cm7 — B♭/D — Gm7

might - y tri - umph o'er His foes. He a -

43

F — Gm — E♭ — B♭/D

rose a Vic - tor from the dark do - main, And He

CD: 26

CD: 53

45

E♭ — C/E — F — F/G

lives for - ev - er with His saints to reign.____ He's a - live,

48
a-live,
a-live
hal-le-lu-jah.
A-live,
C2
B♭2
50
praise and glo-ry to the Lamb.
A-live,
F2
A♭
B♭2
C2
52
a-live,
a-live
hal-le-lu-jah.
A-live
C2
B♭2
54
1
(to meas. 48)
for-ev-er, a-men.
He's a-live,
F2/A
A♭
B♭2
C

*Words and Music Anonymous. Arr.

68
bow, ev - 'ry tongue con - fess That
E♭m7 G♭/A♭ A♭7 D♭ B♭m B♭m/A♭ G♭9 D♭m/F♭
71
Je - sus Christ is Lord;
A♭/E♭ C/E Fm
74
Opt. 3-part
That Je - sus Christ is
D♭m/F♭ A♭/E♭ A♭+/E♭ D♭M7/E♭ E♭
77
Lord.
A♭sus A♭